COLD WAR TEENS

A Book of Short Prose

Carole Claire Ramsay

STEREO A TYPICAL PRESS

STEREO-A-TYPICAL PRESS
Denver, Colorado
www.StereoATypicalPress.com

Copyright © C. Ramsay 2019
All rights reserved.

First printing May 2019

ISBN Number: 978-1-946293-01-5

COVER ART BY: Eglé Gatins Weiland © 2019

Printed in the United States of America

Without limiting the rights under copyright reserved above, no part of this publication may be reproduced, stored in or introduced into a retrieval system, or transmitted, in any form, or by any means (electronic, mechanical, photocopying, recording, or otherwise) without the prior written permission of both the copyright owner and the above publisher of this book.

PUBLISHER'S NOTE
This is a work of fiction. Names, characters, places, and incidents either are the product of the author's imagination or are used fictitiously, and any resemblance to actual persons, living or dead, events, or locales is entirely coincidental.

~Also by the Author~

NOVELS

The God Seed and The Dalai Lama's Wife

The Gates of Athena: Book I, The Empath Series

N'Athenia: Book II, The Empath Series

I, Ngwamba Mae

The Dance of 10,000 Years

Cakes & Ale

SCREENPLAYS & TV

Dancing Backward in High Heels

The Sound of One Man Crying

Driver Wanted

Salem's Revenge

The Ancients

Anguilla Rocks

Code Games

Magdalena's Children

The Cult of Horus

Dedication:

Cold War Teens
Is dedicated to my siblings -
Bill, may you rest in peace,
Ron, Andy, Elaine, Rob and Rick -
Each of whom was also a
Cold War Teen
standing right beside me.

Thank You

I made it through,
because of each of you.

Cold War Teens

These short works of prose were written between 1985-1986
when the author was a high school student.

The contextual concern most present then - Nuclear War - was different from that of today - Climate Change - only in its specifics; for the emotions, the concerns, the struggles, those were the same.

These prose poems have become again, all too relevant for the youth of today not only because of the above concern, but unfortunately because sexism, racism and bias of all kind have re-emerged - a backlash to social progress.

So, I share these pieces now, not to cast an aura of despair, nor to merely remark on how much tragically remains the same, but rather to draw a parallel between our generations and to remind all that this too we shall overcome. It is only a backlash. Evolution in society will prevail.

In so drawing this parallel, it is also my hope that this collection will offer a sense of our shared efforts, and our shared similarities, because none of us should feel alone in our fight, or in our lives.

We all share so much. Humans, of all ages and generations, are much more alike than we are different.

Though the political climate is slightly different, the importance of unity, and the necessity to implement change in the face of a sense of powerlessness, remains much the same.

The Millennials and all the generations which come after you - you all are the hope of tomorrow, the better generations for which we all have striven.

Those coming of age in this new millennia are the hope for us all: that tomorrow may be better than today.

So, I also dedicate this work to you:
Malcolm, Chloe, Tory & Bella, To Danielle & Bradley,
and to ALL those of these brighter generations now and yet to come.

The Beauty Is In the Change

We look from place to place
We search and never find
Something remaining, never changing
From person to person
To spend a life
From place to place
To gather the memories
And like the day, the leaves, the sea,
The beauty is in the change.
But knowing this
We still must search
For that
To surround with our lives
Though day to day
The people, the reasons,
They're gone again
And we must stay and change.

It is not sad,
The beauty is in the change.

The only difference between heaven and hell

Is where you are coming from.

Ω

Until one arrives
At either the top
Or the bottom,
The path leading up,
To one who is drowning,
Looks the same
As the path
Leading down.

War is the final and ultimate admission
of diplomatic incompetence.

Ω

Our military technology has advanced to a stage
where, for the sake of the species, we must
wholeheartedly desire and search for non-military
resolutions to our international conflicts just as we
employ non-military solutions to our domestic
conflicts.

Cold War Teens
A Victory of Sorts
-1986-

The wine was sweet
It flowed freely that day
For there was song
And the guests danced and smiled
Because they were happy.

More Guests came,
Loud and Explosive, their invitations forgotten.
And the question was screamed
Until it was whispered,
Why had they come,
To ruin the day?

And the glasses fell
And the singing stopped.
And the blood of the dancers
Who lay on the carpet
And stared at the ceiling
Was Red
Like the wine,
Which spilled freely
Through the streets
Because it was Red.

-Continued-

And the carpet
And the costumes
Of the dancers
Were stained,
Along with their hopes
And dreams,
Red
A deep, deep Red,
To match their souls.

The wine spilled
From the ruins
Of the church
To form
A reflective pool
At the foot of The Hill
Looking up at The City,
Too late realizing
Its inferiority
Because it was Red

And though the blood
Which flowed thickest
Down The Hill
From The City
To indifferently mingle

-Continued-

With the wine
From the church,
Was also red,

The people
Sitting alone
In The City on The Hill
Told themselves
That they had won.

So, they rejoiced,
Whoever was left,
As best they could,
Without any smiles,
Under the dark, thick clouds,
Though breathing was hard.

The river runs. Shallow and easy, deep and dark. Like life, it runs, continuous, through the dark to the light, through the fear to only the unknown. The river never stops and its only destiny is to run its course whatever that may be, full to the ocean, to the bigger and better, to the fulfillment that lies beyond the end, and makes of it, a beginning. The full knowledge makes death an impossibility.

$$\Omega$$

I know nothing that came before me,

Therefore, I've been alive forever.

$$\Omega$$

Wisdom comes by living in spite of,

undefined by, conditioned perceptions.

Heroes

Heroes
The truly loved America
Democracy,
Liberty,
Freedom
And God.
For those our young grandparents
Would unselfishly ask
To die
A Hero's Death

Heroes
They truly loved America
Destiny
Burden,
And The Proliferation
Of Democracy
For these our young parents asked
Is it necessary, to die a Hero's Death.

Heroes
They truly loved America
Questions,
More Questions,

-Continued-

Communication
And Compromise.
Because of these our young children
Will never need ask,

Why,
  Why,
    Must I take up arms…
      Across the sea…
        In a foreign land…

Heroes
They truly love America

Ω

Ritual can kill a religion

Ω

If timing is everything, then nothing is real

Life transcends appearances because

Appearances are transient

Ω

The nation state is dead.

Ω

To have pride in a place, to be proud to be from a certain piece of land, is a foolishness that has endured too long. It has created barriers and given people reason to set themselves apart, and call themselves different.

Fraternal Islands

Fraternal Islands
Are we all.
Forever
to
Remain
Just
Separated
Brothers.

The Significance

Each word
to the meaning
of a poem
Is insignificant.
Yet, each word is chosen
Precisely,
Exactly,
To be a part of the whole
Because it brings
To the whole
All that it is,
All that it symbolizes.
Good or bad,
It is that way
With our own
Human
Insignificance.

The Eye of a Culture

As I awaken
From the slumber
Of my youth,
I hear, the sounds of sanity.
A child
Pushes a mower
Against the blades of time.
A man
Wipes from his face
The growth of time.
A woman
Erases from forever
Or at least until the night
A wrinkle
In the face of time.
Someone
Cutting down
And then again
Creating,

-Continued-

Forever a cycle,
Never onward,
To stop not time
But their fear
Of that progression.
A child's simple life
Is ended
Before the feet of that forever cycle,
The eye of a culture.

The Skin of My Soul

A child lies dead
Or the altar of life

Her rebellious nature gone,
Simply a memory,

A pain,
A worry,
A caution,
A sorrow,

Lie
In the coffin
Of fear

That was,
I have found,
Just the skin of my soul

-Continued-

A necessary offering, shed,
To give birth
To the me
That was the spirit of that youth.

In-Distinction

And after a rain
I see, or only
Think I see,
An arc of many colors.
But when I look again
I see, or only
Think I see,
That those lines
Those very fine lines
Which mark distinction,

-Continued-

Are hazy
And indistinct.
And that colors
And the shades
Bleed
Into the next
Because of the lines
Of in-distinction.
And so, through that,
which would keep them apart,
Do the colors
Of the arc,
Bleed
One…
Into the other…

The Bridge

I stood on the plank
That was a bridge
And saw myself sinking.

I looked beneath the bridge
And saw the water below.
And all that was between
my feet and the water
was the plank,
on which I stood,
that was a bridge.

I looked to the end
Of the water
And there was land.

That water lapped
at this land
which stretched
in the rising sun.

-Continued-

And all that was between
my feet and the land
was the plank,
on which I stood,
that was a bridge.
I looked beyond the sun
Which played o'er the land
And saw a better day.

And all that was between
myself and the sun
was the darkness,
before the day,
through which I must walk.

I looked beneath the bridge,
And I turned,
Into the sun.

Ambition

Ambition
Of the clever youths
Shall carry them forth
To a better life.
And when they get there
Ambition
Again
Will carry them forth
To a life
That is better yet.
And the search
Never ceasing
Because of
Ambition
Will allow
Those youths
Those products of culture
Never the joy
Of a word or a touch,
Never the peace
of knowing the night.

-Continued-

But the search
In themselves
That gives life to
Ambition
Will lead them on
To a lifetime's work.

An Insignificance

Each person
To another
Has their significance,
That much
We know,
We feel.

These people then
Collect themselves
But not
Oh no
At random.

The differences
That dictate
The lines
And boundaries
Are, they say,
God-given.

We like to think
As we often do
That like a person
These lines,

-Continued-

An entity,
Have some significance.
But then, the feeling
And the thinking done,
The whole
And total
Of us all
Is what shall pass
With the death of a star
And leave the world
To another fate.

The passing of the lines
By the forces
Shall go unnoticed,
Just one more step
Before infinity.

-Continued-

The importance
That whole
Tells itself
It has,
Falls…
Like a hollow laugh…
Before
The power
Of the sea.

To A Mother and A Father

I wanted to bring into you
a small bouquet of flowers,
before I realized,
I was too far away.
Do this for me now,
Pick a bud from your
Garden of many.
Put it, alone, in a vase,
And let it bloom
as you did for me
when you, unselfish,
said nothing
when my life's turning
took me
so far
from you.

Ω

The day I meet someone who makes a first
impression on me that is of any value, I'll
know what being poor is all about.

The End of A Day

A life has quietly slipped away
It has begun a journey
in another way.
We cannot see it, hear it, touch it,
We can but feel its presence.
That part of life now
Is like
The setting of the sun
Into the sea
Which the lovers have watched
And thought beautiful.
It has a purpose,
Oh maddening reason,
To give happiness
And bring
A quiet smile.
The end of life is in
The end of a day,
The end of a storm.

-Continued-

But we who are left behind
Smile at the sky and the rainbow
Yet weep at the one we love most,
Weep at his promise of return
Which has been shown,
In its own way,
To be ... as beautiful.

Trust

Who am I to trust
Is there he to be believed?
Shall I live untrusting
Of my birth right, of my life?
To be untrusting is to live
By self-imposed imprisonment
Locked inside yourself,
Not living of the beauty
That the Greater has provided
And is ours because of trust
One to separate life and trust
Is not found.
Though you be wary,
Trust till you may not,
Live till you may not,
Then, when she who is Greater
Calls and you must go
Say not that you must live
Instead that you have trusted
And have dared to live.

A Life Worth Living

To Live a Life
You Dream a Dream
Yet Die a Thousand Deaths

And yet again,
To Live a Dream,
Does Not Allow For Death

Ω

The *strongest* person in the room is the
one with the strength of her convictions.

Ω

Parenting is by definition
a sad profession,
for the foremost responsibility
of a parent is to give to each child
both the ability and the courage
to leave you.

Something To Believe In

And I believe
Said the man
To the earth
As he bowed
Long and deep
And I believe
Said another
To the figure
On the cross
Far above
Our lowered eyes
And I believe
Said a third
To the wind
As it blew
Without hearing
Or wanting to hear

And I believe
Said I
to myself
Though I be afraid.

The Promise of Shadows

The promise of a haunting
is the light of a new day,
the freedom of comprehension,
the joy of understanding
And yet much more
than with a shadow
is the promise
of a haunting still
that marks you one,
unique and alone
The only promise
of a haunting still.

Foolish But Essential

Foolishly they buy and sell
that which was given
in order that they may improve
that which was perfect.

Foolish, but essential.

A Way of Knowing

I know,
Do I know?
I come
I go
I'm here
And never gone.
The knowing helps not
He's here,
He's there
And he is never gone.
I know
Can I know?
We're here
We're not there.
In my mind
We're never gone.

I cannot know,
It would not help.

Because of this,
I'm never gone.

Commitment

I have given
my heart, my soul, myself.
I have longed
To be requited.
I have missed
with my commitment.
I have known
it is not worthy.
I have committed
and I am married
to that commitment.

Ω

I don't make mistakes,
I don't have regrets
And I don't feel guilty.
I live,
I learn,
And I grow.
It's all a matter of perspective.

The View From This Side

He handed back to me
On that bright day in spring
The final fruition
Of all my work.
And as the sun
Went behind
the clouds,
He remarked
On his gift
Of prophecy.
He knew said he
From behind those wise blinders
As I hung in the balance
From the very beginning
That I
Standing there
Would not understand
The intricacies
Of his meaning
The delicacies of
Their implications
Because
Said he
I am
What
I am
His talk

Was wasted
Fallen deaf

On the ears
Of one
Who
Could not learn

I could see then
Past his wrinkles
And into his youth
And I knew him,
Unequivocably,
Better that himself
Then too
I could see
Into the lives
Of all he head touched
With his words
And his attitudes
As they now moved
No longer reaching
In their circles

Then I
Who had accepted,
Said to he
Who had expected,

We both are wrong.

Truly Civilized

I sit in my room
Alone
And I am thankful
For the walls
For which
I have worked
So hard.

And, as I sit,
I think
Of those
From a culture
Less fortunate
Foolishly they live without
As they sit for hours
Around their fire
In laughing groups
Of unlearned peoples
As ehse dim folks
Talk away
Into the night
The chance for each
To have so much more
From life
Slips away.

And as I listen
To my own laughter
Bouncing back at me
From all sides
I am thankful
For the walls
Which send it
For which
I have worked
So hard.

Ω

I have observed perfection
and I have seen beauty.
And upon closer inspection
I have found
that the beauty
of perfection
is in its flaws.

Ω

You can never be lonely
If you can live with yourself.

Ω

The richest person sees with his ears, feels with his eyes and speaks through his heart.

Ω

In a loving relationship,
what you do for the other,
you do
at no loss
to yourself.

Ω

And those of us
Who think too long
And cry too hard
Are laughed aside
By the wizened tongues
Of the fools gone deaf
As they move to live
Thinking not
'bout all that is lost
As they act
The only catalyst
In their forever progression
Never to reach
The peaceful satisfaction
That belongs to us
Who think too much
Enough not yet
And cry too hard
To see the rainbow.

Love...

The bane and the basis
For life eternally
The question and the answer
Is the meaning
For search, eternally.

$$\Omega$$

I have no need to fly higher and higher,
I need only to fly.

Nothing is real;
The world is open to interpretation

$$\Omega$$

God wants us to forgive our friends and enemies not because we think he'll punish them, but because we know he wouldn't.

$$\Omega$$

Whether or not there is a God should not concern you half so much as the results of that belief.

Ω

A sunset is like old age; It's mellow and rich and makes others happy through its own peaceful strength.

Ω

All problems are trivial if you're at peace with yourself.

Ω

In listening to a person speak of another,
You learn not of the other,
But rather, of the speaker.

A Journey

Enjoy the journey
Do not rush with your tasks
To enjoy the evening,
Enjoy instead, the tasks.
When you find yourself rushing
To a destination of happiness, slow down.
Enjoy instead, the journey.
When you speak, speak not of ideal things,
Enjoy instead, the silence.
If you long for comfort,
Push aside your anxieties
And enjoy instead the dusk
That falls but once a day.
The setting sun, the starless sky,
The newly mown grass
Take advantage of these gifts of the senses,
They may not stay.
And when you look inside yourself,
Long not for what you were not given,
Enjoy instead the journey.

Ω

And the dawn shall come
To follow the night.
Preciously given
To those only
Who've summoned the courage
To face the night.

Ω

I don't want
To follow the wind.
I will do that when I'm dead.

Something To Believe In

And I believe
Said the man
To the earth
As he bowed
Long and deep.
And I believe
Said another
To the figure
On the cross
Far above
His lowered eyes.
And I believe
Said a third
To the wind
As it blew
Without hearing
Or wanting to hear.

And I believe
Said
To myself
Though I be afraid.

One Lone Mind

Though many hellos
And How-do-You-do's
I've handed out
And many I've received,
No man has stopped
Beside my mind
And said,
Myself, I see!
Many today
Have passed the time
Inquireing on my health
Though they be sincere
I'd be much happier
To have but one
Who is able to stop
Beside my mind
And know
This is life,
Let's talk.

When the birds fly, they fly
                         up, up,
Higher and higher. They fly
                                 down, down,
Spiraling, turning
       in the beautiful morning sky.

They fly up
                               and down
                indiscriminately
UP is not
                        better.

Where the birds are soaring to
      Is of no importance
                           compared to the fact
that they
            are soaring.

                Maybe, if people
           weren't so determined that where
               their life is going to
        must be an important part of living,
              then maybe we too…
                   could soar.

Delilah Strong
-short-short fiction-

It was that summer, when the heat shimmered the pavement and Nancy cut all her long hair short and the baby started scratching at her own armpits.

That summer. The summer of heat.

The baby raised her little toddler's arm straight up, the baby did that summer, just enough, halfway to the sky and not all the way. Using the fingers of her other hand, prodding the skin there gingerly and tickling it.

At my Dad's wedding that spring, Grammy had dampened her already overheated wrists and said what a beautiful bride Nancy was. *Angel*, I reminded her. She mumbled then, grumbling at me under her breath, *should have been Nancy*. The old woman added something about a fool.

She's over her survivor guilt now, Nancy tells me, and I try to be happy for this woman who has been so happy for me. But it is the guilt that has made her care so much for me and it is gone now and I am wondering if she will care for me, Sampson's daughter, much longer.

And then the baby reaches up her arm halfway to the sky and it is not my Daddy's baby but the baby loves him all the same and she has cancer; the baby.

It's your baby. It is. Angel is yelling, yelling at my Dad. She is confused, pathetic. I feel sorry. *She is not mine, Angel, but I wish to God that she were.* And my Dad's three-month marriage is on the rocks.

Nancy has cut the luck from her head and it is gone, along with her strength, to the place of her survivor guilt. I go to her, to the hospital where she is with her daughter only I want to be her daughter, to have her time, even now, in the midst of illness. This is the selfishness of me.

She wrings her hands. I hold her shoulder. My dad walks in.

Angel is pregnant now and the mortgage has come due; Nancy's. *I've been mostly keeping up since Jacob's accident, but...* She doesn't know I have heard. I peek out from Nancy's bathroom at the sound of her words stopping. Not my presence that has stopped them, my dad's lips. He is holding her now, in her kitchen and I close the door and Angel's child, not my father's either.

The end of the summer nears now though the temperature soars on and no leaves fall. The baby struggles, yet she is strong. She can win. But her mother has cut her hair. This summer, the summer of heat, she has cut it all off short and the baby turns, takes a turn for the worst and Angel has run out.

The first leaves turn, the baby is gone, gone to the place of her mother's hair and the summer of heat. The survivor guilt though, it stays behind. *It has come back for me dear,* Nancy tells me when our visit ends, *you understand, you must.* She apologized then and when I leave, I know she too is gone, gone from my life.

My dad is crying. The snow is flying. Sampson's strength was in Delilah's hair, not his own. Sampson's daughter, I, strong or weak, capable or not, am alone now. No heated summer or shortened hair or survivor guilt will return Sampson's strength to me. He too withers, thin like the winter snows that year.

Shriveled leaf from majestic oak, he falls, the last of autumn against hard scrabble of ice that once too, was soft as snow.

Sampson's daughter, Delilah strong, I pin back my hair and alone I stand.

The Best Book Ever Written
An Essay

All Quiet on the Western Front, Gone With the Wind, Love in the Time of Cholera, For Whom the Bell Tolls?

Haven't Guessed? The book that has it all to take this title was written by a Dr. Theodore Geisel. When he wrote *Horton Hears A Who,* he called himself Dr. Seuss and had been known for books of rhyme and clever silliness for many years.

He chose simple language and brevity as media for expression and because he did so and then added delightful, fanciful illustrations, it was assumed that the sole audience for this book — both actual and intended — was children. It was in his best interest for marketing the book, so Ted Geisel allowed the assumption to stand. What is in this small narrative however, falls far from reaching its potential if read only by the age-limited. What is it about this storyline that compels one so?

Simply this: *Horton Hears A Who* has the agenda of an existential treatise. No analysis of existence that we have – not from Kierkegaard, Camus, Nietzsche, Sartre, or any – can be said to be any finer in its conceptualization of the issues around that subject. In Horton's journey to save a small Who village atop a rounded puffball weed, Seuss explores whether the Whos actually exist. Beyond that, he explores such concepts as the right to existence as well as what constitutes sufficient proof of that existence and to whom.

Horton then, as he travels, discusses with himself what one's possible *responsibilities* toward another's existence might be when that life intersects with one's own. When Horton begins to question whether size matters in relation to that existential intersection and responsibility, he is turning the book toward three microcosms simultaneously. The first is that of the parent-child relationship, and the second is that of human being to all other species. The third, if size is thought of as economic or military size, becomes equally obvious: that of the hegemon to all the other nations of the world, of the developed nation to the developing nations.

But Horton wants no more for his globe-like weed and its inhabitants (perhaps metaphorically, the inhabitants of the world's developing nations) that that they be let alone to live in peace without the hawkish, aggressive, and very much destructive interference of the monkeys and vultures of the story (perhaps the so-called 'developed' nations) who team up to torture and ultimately end the Whos and their village – the existence of which they purport not to accept. Interesting to this analyst is the intensity of the degree to which these characters were moved to utterly destroy that in which they feared to believe.

Seuss' volume that returns to its philosophical roots albeit in a different channel when it becomes clear what it is that will actually end the doubt in the minds of vultures and moneys and will allow them to believe without fear. In a succinct and miniature version of historical philosophical debates around the world, it is the *senses* of the vulture-monkeys which does it for them. When they can *hear* the Whos, they can then and only then, believe in their existence (and allow themselves to be kind to them.) It was not enough that someone else had heard the Whos, for they could feel complete comfort in telling themselves that Horton, the sensitive being hearing things they couldn't hear, was not sane like them – and of course, then torture him too.

Interesting as well is the petition toward democracy represented in the fact that the Whos could not be heard until every single one of them including the last, tiny, young Who was calling out loudly and strongly and in unison. Every single individual voice was important in the globe-weed of Seuss' Who world.

Existential analysis, biblical recapitulation, parenting guide book, narrative on international relations, and historical philosophical debate – I ask you, what other volume has so much on offer in such brief and simple words?

Habit & Wisdom
Essay in Three Parts © 2006

What is that one difference, that intangible something that has you reacting well one day and yet the very next, reacting poorly to a situation deeply similar?

That difference is tension and wisdom, maturity and habit. For instance, the morning runs smoothly and you're aces at work. Lose your cool with your kids' puttsing preparations for school, however, and suddenly no one around you seems to be capable of driving and co-workers seem to have lost I.Q. points overnight. Then, there it is, you find yourself tearing into a now "idiotic" colleague while up in the corner of the room near the ceiling, some piece of you floats, wondering surreally what happened to the calm you inhabited yesterday.

We could talk about habit now. We could talk about being totally, completely asleep inside of your cocoon of habits and about how behavioral consistency could increase but that would have to begin with awareness and you can't gain that while mired in the habits that, while they may have at one time helped you to survive, are now, also holding you back, keeping you from thriving.

To venture beyond your cocoon of habit and safety, your zone of comfort, though, you would need first to *see* it. You would have to see *reactions* instead of responses and habits where wisdom might one day reside.

What we are talking about though, is how maybe that *is* what wisdom is - one of three aspects of wisdom anyway. That maybe allowing yourself, *causing* yourself to wait until all the habits and reactions have coursed through your body and then to wait more, until a *response* has formed, maybe that is wisdom.

Seeing it, suddenly there it is, the wisdom manifested by responding instead of reacting.

Beyond the personal scale in which we maximize individual self-development, there is a grander problem with these human struggles. That is this – what does this lack of self-awareness, this absence of reflection and wisdom which leaves a person flailing inside their cocoon of 'safety' do to us when on the scale of *nations*?

Maybe that's what a leader should be (and by definition is?) Leader - a person exemplifying the wisdom to wait and the wisdom to gather a response, before acting. What a world we would have, by that definition! Leaders, basing action upon transparent and analyzable thought processes over instantaneous, spontaneous, emotional rejoinder? It would be a world of wisdom.

When the world's leaders are, instead of wise and *responsive*, asleep at the wheel and *reacting* from habit, unaware even of the difference, what then? Security means fighting, it means armies and weapons. What else could it mean, right? What happens to our world then, when its leaders react without pause or reflection, introspection or wisdom, when *their* reactions are every bit as reflective of groggy sleep-ful-ness (and not sleep*i*ness) as the anonymous road-rager one car over, what then?

Wisdom, The 2nd Aspect
Part 2 of 3

Wisdom. How does one define it? Does the definition differ from culture to culture, or are all humans really valuing the same traits when they use the label *wisdom*? As I have searched for actions described by this term among a vast array of world cultures, the idea has developed in me that what is meant is not only in fact deeply similar, but also that it can best be summed up with a three-pronged definition. Three prongs which encompass three aspects to what I think of as The Sophic Triad. The first of these three prongs of wisdom was the topic discussed last week. That dimension to the concept of wisdom regarded the ability to see and move forward from you Comfort Zone, to realized that what kept you safe and helped you survive is now keeping you from thriving. Seeing that, one works to move past this package of habits and to develop the wisdom to allow all reaction to course through your body and pass, and then to wait longer while an actual response forms before one acts on a concern.

Let us add to that now, the second aspect of the triad. Wisdom, we can say, is also the act of living in spite of conditioned perceptions.

You live eighteen years (or more) with a given group of people we label family. Within that family, you are conditioned toward the interpretation of acts and events through a given perspective. To remain always after that in the many years to come, still interpreting the whole world through your own small familial perspective is beyond limiting. It is narrow and proximate and is contributing, though you don't see it, to cognitive dissonance inside of you – a dissonance that may be at the root of your self-medicating, your addiction, your internal pain or simply your absence of mindfulness when most you want it. For it is in fact, those people who were taught to think one way about a group of people but who *do not*, who have wisdom and life insights in abundance. It is the ACT of living in spite of those perceptions conditioned by youth and family which is the visible marker of the presence of wisdom.

Isn't that what the inclusion of the study of liberal arts into an education is really all about?

Isn't the point of that part of one's university or self-education to try to open a mind *beyond* the one set of perceptions that make up a single world perspective and let (or force) in multiple other perspectives? This inclusion – of history, literature, philosophy, ethics, anthropology – is there because it undergirds our belief that no one can or should be considered educated unless capable of seeing beyond one's own immediate, familial perspective.

Carved into the marble over the entrance to Norlin Library on the Boulder campus of the University of Colorado are the words, "He who knows only his own generation, remains always a child." The concept (unlike the words) is not limited to a single gender, but reflects instead the value humanity places on holding multiple perspectives on life at the same time. The link between that capacity and maturity is so strong as to be defining.

Around the world, humans value the wisdom to wait to respond *and* they value the wisdom to check that response through not a single, but a variety, of interpretive perspectives. In other words, they value the second dimension of Wisdom - living in spite of conditioned perspectives.

There is No Short-Term, Throw Out Self-Interest Too
Wisdom Essay, Part 3

Last week we re-capped here, the first of the three prongs of wisdom's triad while adding to it, the second. This week, let's bring it all home by looking at the last of the three aspects which describe The Sophic Triad.

The first of the three dimensions of the concept that is wisdom was described as the wisdom to wait to respond (physically, emotionally, verbally) until all reactions had coursed through your body and passed. The second dimension described wisdom as the act of living in spite of conditioned perceptions.

To complete the three-dimensional picture of wisdom, we look to the arc of time as it relates to the view of life we choose to hold.

In the short-term, one can *rationalize.* Humans can rationalize *anything*! We can convince ourselves that stealing money or time from another, for instance, or restricting the movement and economic mobility of others, are acceptable acts because: they deserve it;

they would just do it to me; it is the will of some 'God;' Someone else will just take advantage if I don't; this is how nature intended him/her/them to be…etc, etc. The list is endless because like human imagination and ingenuity, our ability to rationalize to ourselves about acts we want to do, is also endless.

It is by *thinking* more broadly that we can *act* from a point of wisdom, overcoming innate tendencies toward rationalization. Think about what your act (or thought) will mean for people Seven Generations from now as the Iroquois do. In fact, most indigenous and even European cultures also think in terms much longer and broader than do people born in the U.S. Is this because our society itself is younger? Perhaps. Either way, to actualize this idea, remember: There is no short-term. Throw out self-interest too.

In this way, through rationalization, one can in the short-term worry about labels and convince oneself not only that your personal bad behavior is acceptable, but that bad behavior on a world scale is also acceptable. That it is, in fact, unavoidable.

Protecting the world's temperature, soil, air and water while also making a profit you tell yourself via this short-term lens incompatible, the destruction unavoidable. It is only with a long-term lens monitoring one's reflection that a person quickly recognizes that these two ideas are not only compatible, *they are inseparable. They are the same option.*

It is with a short-term lens that one also falsely perceives one's self-interest as *in opposition to* another's self-interest (zero-sum.) It is only via the long-term lens that such a fallacy is spirited away like dust before the sun, allowing recognition to dawn regarding the inseparable interdependence of people's interests, indeed of the interests of all the world's peoples – that there is in fact, no such thing as *self*-interest.

Wouldn't that be something, huh. In America? One more alcoholic taking his first step on the road of facing his addiction (and all that lies beneath it) because the impact on his children's children's children will be profound? One less young family succumbing to the peer pressure of the status quo, and living instead within their budget, or perhaps even as minimalists, because again the impact has sky-high potential?

And then again, how about our 'regular guy' at the helm? How about instead of one more scheme to make himself richer (in the least valuable of ways to be rich,) s/he chooses instead an action and a path of actions which makes us ALL, and our descendants *truly* safer, maybe wiser, and in *this* way, very wealthy indeed.

In the end, there is no short-term, and throw out self-interest too.

The Three Faces of Voice

Elizabeth Parks and her husband, Sean Taylor, were having some confusion around an upcoming trip they were planning together for their vacation. It was not unlike other confusions they'd experienced in the past – sometimes around trips but also even around smaller decisions. Misfired connection loomed for them around the bigger, ephemeral, intangible parts of life as well – leaving them both feeling a bit disconnected from each other in a way they couldn't quite name.

What they were missing out on having in their lives and in their connection, and what was keeping them further apart than they could otherwise be, was what I call, the Three Faces of Voice. Voice is just the desire to be heard though, isn't it? Wrong.

Voice consists of these three aspects working together:

1. The honor of being heard,
2. The honor of being allowed to listen, and
3. The true intimacy, connection, and understanding that voice sharing creates.

When Sean was thinking about the various smaller decisions that go into making up their trip together, he was falling victim to a mental trick that can happen when we are less than diligent in our attention – he was thinking things through and making decisions in his own mind, without Elizabeth and with limited information. He was then compounding the problem by sharing with Elizabeth information on the decision he'd arrived at, only about half the time. Much of the time, he'd not even been aware he'd arrived at decisions. This mental processing without full awareness and without input from others who would be affected by the resulting decisions is a problem even when the person doing it believes they've included some of the likes and dislikes of the other(s) in the process.

It is a problem because what got left out was Elizabeth's right to be heard, Sean's right to honor her by allowing her to hear his thinking, and the greater communication and intimacy they would have arrived at for having shared the process of decision-making – and its preliminary steps of information gathering – together.

On their own, neither one has all the information he or she needs to make the right decisions anyway. He, or she, may feel he is selecting, for instance, the *right* morning of the vacation to hire the snorkel boat as he plans away, given that he knows his wife. He feels good about this. If however, unknown to him, Elizabeth has promised the children the same morning for a jungle tour, frustration abounds. This is only the least challenging example. Other examples get into issues of identity and dehumanization. By talking it through, both parties, *all* parties, have *all* the information they need to make all the right decisions. This is what I call, Collaborative Solution Creation. It is far superior to compromise because it gets *all* the information – and the stories behind that information – on the table and into the decision making process where it can help to create not just passable, mediocre solutions, but solutions that maximize total success. Besides, it's just more fun this way, working, playing, together, hearing the stories behind the data. Both the results and the process then, are superior to other forms of decision making and communication.

It is sometimes challenging enough for people to understand that when they have wronged another, the other, at times, wants nothing more than one aspect of *voice* – the right to talk about what happened to him and how it made him feel. From there, it can be further challenging to understand that sometimes, it is only the right to listen, the honor to be allowed to hear, that is being desired – and in its absence is harming those about whom one cares.

And even that can be a new and different idea – honoring someone? By letting them in on *my* thoughts? That is exactly right, exactly what you *are* doing, when you let someone hear what you think, when you let them into the process. Sean had no idea he was hurting Elizabeth by not talking with her, how surprising for him then, when he realized that he could honor her by this sharing – and began thinking *that* way.

Interestingly, hearing your own thoughts out loud, and hearing the thought process itself, will often also improve both. So that in addition to the benefit of honoring another, you have also gained the benefit of strengthening your own thinking – and the process that thinking goes through – all by speaking it out loud with a trusted other in attendance.

There is yet one more benefit that this single, simple change can bring. We already know it can cause others around you to feel honored instead of left out, and as a decision-maker in their own destiny instead of spectator to it and that for the speaker him/herself, speaking the thought process out loud can strengthen both the thinking and the process. The last benefit is that it brings two companions closer than they were already, and deepens the trust. It does this not just through the honor and participation – though those do help – but also through the intimacy of knowing another's thoughts and through the opportunity to understand the *whys* behind the decisions and the pieces of each decision. The *whys* are the person's stories, the experiences that affected her causing her to be who she is today. And knowing these stories in a way that is deeper and more connected than simply hearing about them in an anesthetized and one-dimensional telling across a wide table, creates that.

By hearing about it in the present, in the moment and the immediate, with all the 'alive-ness' and dynamism that contributes, Elizabeth and Sean can both begin to feel a connectedness, and a living *experience* of the other's experience and not just an understanding of it. Then develops, over time, a special kind of a trust; the kind of trust one gains by knowing another won't be off in one direction, alone, choosing actions which will affect both.

How great that relationship became – for Elizabeth and Sean - but also with their friends, work colleagues and families - that yesterday was marked by confusion, sadness, and vague disconnection but is today marked instead, through sharing aloud the Three Faces of Voice, by a feeling of being heard, respected, honored, and of the deep feeling of trust and of sharing *truly* intimate knowledge of another – and the more durable threads of connection those intimacies shared create.

Primary Emotions, Secondary Emotions

Joy, coming as it does, filled with laughter that bubbles up, perhaps as we are surrounded by loved ones…and fear, these are real. These are examples of *primary* emotions. The latter might even be called more of a valuable, physiological response to survival dangers than an actual emotion. Sadness too, is primary. These are natural, normal, and very healthy. There is not a problem with these or with the short-term experience of them.

Human problems begin to form only when, for external reasons, these natural, healthy responses to life are deemed less than acceptable and, as a result, become repressed instead of experienced. Fear, for instance, might be deemed, from an early age and by influential others such as parents and later, peers, as a "less-than-manly" experience. In being incorrectly labeled as such, the healthy and quite appropriate response, fear, begins to get repressed, subverted. In its stead we find something quite manufactured, quite unhealthy, and deeply inappropriate; a *secondary* or derived emotion. Not real. Created. All so that the correct response to a frightening situation doesn't make us feel that our solid and unwavering femininity or masculinity might waver.

This secondary or derived emotion that surfaces to replace fear is anger.

Yes, that's right. Anger is derived. It is an inappropriate response that comes from the repression of fear, an appropriate response. It can also be a secondary emotion for sadness, like the sadness from injustice.

As was discussed in an earlier paper though, culture is that which helps us to adapt *more* successfully to the environment in which we find ourselves. This then, is an example of an illogical application of what is sacredly referred to as, culture. Culture can and should be changed, all the time. Its purpose is to aid, not stifle, human adaptation. More importantly, we should recognize, through this definition, that not all things currently protected under the sacred umbrella of culture need be protected – for they are not culture.

The purpose of discussing culture's true aim and of discussing the primary emotions and the secondary emotions is that by so labeling and discussing them, we hope to bring them out of hiding and into the light of day. It is hoped then that regular people going about their regular lives can more easily begin to recognize when their own responses to situations before them have deviated from the path of healthy response into the terrain of secondary, unproductive, inorganic response. Greater recognition is of course, an end goal in itself, but in creating greater, faster recognition in the every day, it is more likely that the damaging, derived secondary "emotion" can be stopped – and in being stopped, prevent you from creating in your own life, a vast empire of damage and fallout.

Institutionalized Non-Violence

Violence…It's not a habit…

…nor is it an inborn human trait

about which we can do nothing.

5 of the 6 factors that cause conflict to
become violent are economic in nature

…not religious…

…not ethnic…

Non-violent response to conflict is *chosen*.

It is chosen when and where exist the

economic and **infrastructural** means

to allow conflict to resolve non-violently.

That is…

>Where the civil institutions

for grievance resolution exist at all levels, there too,

non-violence exists.

Peace…

>It's not the Absence of War,

>But the Presence of Justice

after that, it is the ***Institutionalization of Justice***

Did You Know…?

2017

Recently a friend gave voice to a question that is likely in the minds of many across our country at this time: Has this focus on sexual assault become a witch hunt? An ironic choice of term given that the original witch hunts were also misogynistic and sought out only powerful, female community leaders and their allies.

The alternative reality – that the full extent of sexual assault, harassment and bias in our society crosses every socioeconomic line, pervades every industry sector, and *can never be fully known* – is anathema, indeed incomprehensible, to so many Americans. The answer to my friend's question is, sadly, no, it is not a witch hunt, not even close.

Sadder still is that we haven't even yet exposed the rock-bottom whole truth, the full breadth and depth of the problem of sexual assault, harassment and stereotypes. It is in fact pandemic and endemic to the structure of our system. It is a part, perhaps a key part of a system. These interlocking aspects of intractability are, indeed, what make a system a *system*, it is that which defines a problem as a *systemic problem*.

Kids sports, adult sports, boy scouts, religions, commercial real estate, oil & gas industry, politics, finance, banking, mining, college (students and faculty), Hollywood… None of these are immune to the ravages of assault, or of sexism, and the economic assault that sexism silently imparts on women's careers and earning potential.

Just as the greater portion of evil is banal, the banality of sexism defines it as the greater evil over its relative, misogyny. "I could hire you but my wife would kill me." "We want to hire *you,* but we *have* to hire him, after all he's going to be somebody in this industry someday." "Who will watch your kids?" "When do you plan to get pregnant?" "I've arranged for you to go away with me for the weekend to my Aspen home." "We'd love you for our PSA, but you're going to need to do a nude shower scene for us first." "LGBT rights are the last civil rights issue!" All of these statements are versions of the same problem. One might like to think I am going to say they are also things that have been said to a group of women I know. The truth is worse – they are statements that have all been made to only *one* woman - me. This is in fact, only a *small portion* of the incredible statements, assumptions and beliefs that this one specific woman has had to hurdle during her life and career, and that isn't including the instances of actual assault at work. Contemplate the true extent of the reality of the problem if every woman has to face, and hurdle, so many injustices. Each one represents a significant and added hurdle in a career, and they happen to women *every day* and in *every area of life*. It is incomprehensible to fully perceive how pervasive is the injustice.

Sexual assault, sexual harassment, off-color jokes, and stereotypes that 'inform' anyone's concept of what a person *should* be because of her/his gender are not different problems, they are different placeholders along the **same** problem; three bars, one hurdle. Men's careers have hurdles too. Women's careers just have more. Men have to work hard, women have to work harder. It is not only unjust, it is one of the most extensive, pervasive and *systemic* injustices of our time.

Worse too is that only a small percentage – the tip of the proverbial iceberg – of the hurdles that women face in life and in their careers are verbalized. Most of these will negatively impact their careers without the individual ever even being told, and often without the relevant stereotype ever even being stated out loud. It is incredibly difficult to refute an assumption that is never verbalized.

Are men being blamed for being male and 'witch hunted' for sexual assault and harassment? Oh, so sadly, the answer is a resounding NO. The truth is the reverse, that for generations, women have been blamed for being female and men have been allowed to get away with behaviors that are beneath them, often never having realized that they themselves were better than that and deserved more too. For assault, harassment and stereotypes destroy the perpetrators as much as they destroy the victims. Men, like women, are just better off when we are all equal, and like women, men too live a fuller, richer life when we are all seen as simply… human.

Did You Know…
Daycare is not a Women's Issue

2001

Working Mother magazine cites day care as a leading issue among 'working' mothers (as if there were such a thing as a non-working parent.) In the corporate world, new and continuing attention is being paid to the provision of daycare services because of 'the number of mothers now in the workforce.'

Women's issues however, are things like equal training, equal opportunity, equal representation in government and equal pay. Women's issues can be said to be things like the assurance of equal freedoms, safety from assault, harassment and stereotypes, free will and personal agency, and control over our own bodies. Since we humans cannot seem to rise above judging each other, a woman's issue includes ensuring that we are, at least, all judged by the same rule set. It is also in the category of women's issues to ensure equal reproductive *responsibility*.

Daycare however, cannot be said to be in the category of items labeled women's issue because it is, far more importantly, a *family* issue. It applies equally to fathers. Fathers cannot be productive employees without knowing they have good care for their children. On the flip side of the same coin, they cannot be successful dads if they are required to be always at work (which in turn will make them less productive employees.)

The absence of care for children, be it provided by a parent, a workplace, or through compensated outside providers, would place males in the *same* situation as their female counterparts.

In Europe where *families* are the priority, and an honest priority at that, companies have for decades provided on-site daycare as well as daycare compensation. More importantly, they have also provided the many flexible alternatives which help both parents to spend more hours in the home, raising their own children. In support of the entire family, European corporations offer arrangements such as job sharing, flex hours, work from home, and extended paternity leave. The latter being an oddity in this country, one still struggling with maternity leave and still unclear as to the importance of fathers.

And that is where the problem lies. Parenting is partnering. When the man is home with the children, it's not babysitting, it's still parenting. There is no part of families which is a women's issue. Children and families, these are societal issues. The having of a uterus does not make women more capable parents. When my children were born, I did not somehow have an instruction manual for them that was more clear or more available to me than to my husband. Babies simply don't come with instructions. End of discussion. Neither new parent knows exactly what to do and both struggle equally. How a society will rise to aid in that struggle will reflect in the present and well into the future, not on women, but on the society which did or did not support those parents.

Men's roles have changed. They changed for the same reason behind all change - because change was necessary. Needs were going unmet under the old system - for children, for women, and for men - and unmet need, *that* is what makes change necessary.

Defining daycare correctly as a family and societal issue and not as a women's issue is reflective of this change. Like all terminology changes, this one too can help alter erroneous thinking while also improving behavioral response – that is, improving the *solution*.

Societally helping men to take on their own responsibilities and not passing them off onto a woman or onto anyone else, this is the shift that is needed. With this single shift we can stop men from impregnating teen girls and then calling the teenaged children the problem. We can help women to achieve some of their own dreams and to earn what they are worth while making them better and happier parents and partners. We can help children feel greater stability and support and decrease their, currently inevitable, sense of cognitive dissonance on recognizing sizeable fractures between their understanding of life and their personal experience in the home.

But, as in all our current shifts, the greatest winners are men. This is because in all our current shifts in thinking and resulting behavior, men get to grow - they get to fully experience emotion and a full life instead of a life under Toxic Masculinity. They get to be mature and responsible and held accountable as women are; to be a parent in all its glory and challenge instead of a sperm donor. They get to be not just synonymous with their work title, but to be instead a full, rich, complete human. There is nothing more beautiful than that. It is all of *that* which society harvests by realizing that daycare is not an issue that belongs to women.

Naïveté

It was my smile he disliked. This friend of a friend. Every time he saw me, he said, I was smiling. Life isn't that good, he'd say, did I think it was all roses and peaches and cream? Now, that's a foolish question to ask while staring at the pacemaker of a 32-year-old woman. No, I said quietly, I didn't think that. But the smile remained.

In my work I communicate with high-ranking decision makers of this and other countries, almost all of whom are, perhaps surprisingly, pretty good people trying to do what is right. Many of these though are also terrified and allowing their choices to rise from this fear.

Ideologically, there are a large percentage of these decision makers who fall into the same belief as my friend of a friend - that anyone who chooses calmness, peace or sound decision making over fear, is simply naïve and doesn't understand the depth of the situation. Those who believe this, miss the courage in such a choice, they miss seeing both the free agency involved and the immense strength required in continuing with such a choice.

What if law makers, decision makers and leaders also made such a powerful, strength-based choice? What if, fear *wasn't* the basis for deciding on, for instance, foreign policy choices?

Arriving at the *best* solutions and policies, the *right* solutions and policies requires one to think - clearly, logically, fairly. Thinking - any thinking - is not a possible result of fear though. Violence, aggression and oppression - these are the results of fear, the *only* possible results of fear.

But violence doesn't resolve issues. Let me say that twice. Violence… does NOT … resolve issues. Thinking that it can is not only truly naïve, it's actually insane. What sort of world would we create if leaders led not from fear but from the sort of strong inner peace that enables one to stare into the face of fear and come up with the *right* policy, the fair and just policy? Not war, not aggression and oppression, but a pathway forward - a true and stable pathway forward - what world then, were leaders thusly able?

Neither smiling nor calmly and without fear selecting the right pathway or policy are happenstance. They are each a choice. They are there, present in a person's life, not out of happenstance, but out of *intention*.

Smiling into the face of death, darkness, or war and seeing a way clear to something better, something *smarter*, these are the only true choices we actually have in life. This is what we *can* put intention behind and have choice over. Not so much control, do we have, over ill health, corrupt business partners, or the over-the-top greed of corporate moguls unregulated by government. It is only the *response*, in each case, that is ours to choose. Will I, a citizen or law-maker, in a misguided but sincere attempt to protect myself look at the world in a way that creates more of the fear I perceive? Or will I walk straight through whatever version of the valley of shadows that may or may not surround me and choose instead to collaborate with the very 'others' I may fear?

Strength comes in many forms. The inner variety, and the behaviors and possibilities that arise from it, will not only never be naïve, it will in fact always be the only version of strength that will ever matter in our world and its hope for a future.

The Best Relationship Book Ever Written
An Essay

The Art of Loving? Kama Sutra? Keeping the Love You Find? Give up? It's none of these. Shel Silverstein's thin volume marketed largely to an audience of children, *The Big O Meets the Missing Piece,* is the book which in the simplest use of language depicts the true essence of a healthy, mature relationship. The very prevalence of relationship books (there are 20,000 titles listed on Amazon alone. There are over forty *categories* for relationship improving titles. The worst of these, *by far*, is John Gray's, *Men are From Mars…,* but that's a separate essay,) informs us of the overwhelming lack of success in human relationships. It also indicates the intensity of the *desire* for healthy, strong relationships among the human creature.

But if that is true, then what is this missing ingredient in relationships which people all over are feeling the absence of and cannot always generate or even name. Is it affection? Attention? Love? Joy? What is this seemingly holy and unattainable grail?

As the Missing Piece, in the shape of a pie wedge, sits idly, it waits for its Other to fit itself into. It searches high and low for one into which it will fit just right. Many 'Others,' of various shapes, weights, and capacities arrive but The Missing Piece never fits one just right for very long. It even tries to make itself subjectively 'more attractive' before realizing it may be scaring away or repelling the one true Other into which it would fit most well. Besides, one Other comes along who takes only the 'attractive' bits of The Piece, ignoring the more important, substantive parts of it. The Piece keeps moving along, searching, and learning and trying. In the end, The Piece finds one Other who is whole, and in being whole, simply rolls along beside The Piece through life.

What Silverstein's take reminds us of in this simple way with just a circle and a pie wedge is that what is missing from so many human connections is actually something that *a relationship cannot give*. Whole people – that is what is missing. Each individual has got to BE whole, on their own and prior to intimacy, and contribute a complete person to each relationship. The absence of the lovely aspects to life listed above (affection, joy, love…) is only a symptom. It is a symptom that cannot be remedied by people seeking others through whom to mask their shortcomings. *Every person* must do the work – to face their fears, strengthen their shortcomings, create healthy boundaries, and respect themselves enough to demand respectful, kind behaviors of those they spend time with. Each person must understand they alone have *and deserve* the right to CHOOSE who they spend time with and they must alone do the work necessary to rise to that level of understanding.

One must be comfortable with and loving of one's own self. Once that is underway, the intangible goals of life which in their absence are symptoms will come to you. They will not come easily; people will force you to defend your healthy boundaries and choices, will attempt to persuade you that you don't deserve or have the right to these healthy choices. But, with courage enough to face the hurdles and build healthy choices into one's life, and strength enough to enforce them, joy and love *will come.*

The irony is that they won't come in the way so many expect – as a by-product of intimacy – but the other way around, as a by-product of loving yourself and as a prelude to intimacy.

But to do this one must *also* walk the fine line at the other extreme, the one between healthy boundaries and self-centeredness. Nothing good can come of that extreme either, any more than at the first extreme – of giving so generously that one fails even to include one's own safety and happiness in the equation. It is the middle land, the balance in between all extremes and living inside of *that*, which reaps the harvests. The humble ink line drawings of this text address this idea as well. The Big O rolling along, does not cry out about its own self, about its successes or capacities. The need for this, in one who like the Big O is truly whole, simply does not exist. The Big On does not need anything *from* the pie wedge, does not need recognition or adoration. It does not need to fit into it, or vice versa. The Big O is not even waiting for the pie wedge to develop into an O itself. It is not waiting for (or wanting) anything at all. It is simply being. The Big O only suggests to The Missing Piece that perhaps, if it so chose, it could roll along by itself. A modest insight and not a lecture, that is one indication the Big O avoided this second pitfall, that of egoism, in its own healthy development. In being willing to have another roll along beside it, we learn as well that it does not *require* aloneness either. It is in rolling along, metaphorically doing its work on *self*-development, that The Missing Piece first wore down its sharp pie-wedge edges and then slowly transformed its shape – it became a circle, a whole, a Big O, of its own.

There is, the book tells us in its closing pages, one more potential pitfall. It is not, the ink drawings say, solely the ability and the willingness to develop oneself despite the constant temptation to be a tool in someone else's life (or demand the same of another.) It is also the capacity to be willing to roll along *beside another* which is important. Required Isolation and healthy self-development are antithetical. Being *able* to be alone and be comfortable is incredibly important. *Needing* to avoid other humans is a deep limitation. Again we see, that it is the land in between the two extremes, the land of balance, where self-development lives. Along with affection, joy, beauty, love, happiness, might not another by-product of wholeness, of self-development be that – the comfort in sharing, in being able to humbly roll alone and to be accepting of other Wholes humbly rolling along nearby?

Being Whole without being self-centered, or the observe too isolated, what more could any single non-experiential media possibly give us with which to better understand such intimately *experiential* phenomena as our healthy selves, our healthy development, and the creation of healthy, mature human relationships?

AFTERWORD

*An Essay by
Delia LaJeunesse,
Founder, Stain'd Arts & Magazine*

On December 27th 2018 the night sky in Queens, NYC turned blue. Electric blue. Beautiful blue, reflected on a white canvas of cloud. Observers took to Twitter speculating about alien invasions, terrorist attacks. It was later learned to be a high voltage electrical explosion at a nearby power plant.

I assume that by the time this is being read, most of us will have forgotten this. This is how it goes, these days. We are inundated. We hear of crises multiple times a day, and through multiple mediums. The messages come loud and urgent and they heighten everything. But also, they numb, and leave us in a state of general unease without any clear source. Naturally, these stories, these blips in our collective consciousness, are soon forgotten. We can only hold so much.

To be clear, this was not a crisis. Not even close. Though it was a certainly a phenomena for all those looking out the window that night, seeing the sky a wild color, watching it all flicker and flame. I think it was a moment of realization – of realizing how small you would be in the unlikely occurrence of an extraterrestrial event, a bomb, a nuclear explosion, a shooting. This is where our minds go.

Reflecting on this in the days following, on the specific fears that people in the five boroughs had on that night, brought to mind my mother's friend. The friend mused about how she used to write comedies and horror stories in high school. She'd write about nuclear bombings, about nuclear war, about total annihilation. She said, "Horror movies more than anything are a reflection of our generation. I was never terrified of zombies, just nuclear war." She laughs and it is funny, sort of, but it's also a fascinating observation. What are the fears of my generation and how are they presented in the media we consume?

I remember one summer night, asleep in the desperate heat of my apartment, with the windows wide open, a transformer blew. The bang was so loud I woke up clutching and panicked and called several people. I am not a nervous person, I feel generally quite calm and rather intuitive. I'd like to think I'd know when a sound is really bad. But sounds like these do startle, especially in an age of lockdown drills and car bombs, and sensibilities aside, my heart was pounding.

When I wake from dreams of the end of the world—where there is no water, or the medicine has gone bad on us, or there is no more space left, between us—I cannot immediately sleep again. On this night, too, it took me a while to get myself back to sleep after I resolved that all was well because, though nobody answered my phone call, the media was not reporting anything, and there were no sirens.

Which is itself an interesting way to note a crisis. When the real catastrophe hits, will the reporting be accurate? Will there be a siren?

There is no siren now.

I do not really fear a terrorist attack, or being caught in a shooting. The real thing I fear, the thing that poses such catastrophic danger my brain probably can't conceptualize it, is the warming of our planet, the flooding, the displaced people, the accumulation of plastic. The thing about the environmental degradation we are experiencing today is how silent, how unseen, how subtle it is. It hangs there, sometimes palpably, like on dry summer evenings, on warm winter days, when the air conditioner breaks down, or the car runs out of gas. It is there, lingering, in those moments. Mostly though, it is not obtrusive. It is not loud, it is not immediate, its dangers are hard to grasp. It does not call for sirens, and if it did they would be so ongoing we would numb to this, too.

Which I suppose brings me to the few sirens that there are. There were sirens in the summer of 2017 when the West was on fire and the South was flooding. Though, these sirens spoke of immediate evacuation, not of the dangers of our lifestyles, and they did not persist as they perhaps ought to have.

I really am generally calm. Yet I'd be lying if I said I was always this way, or that I think it's always better this way. Sometimes I worry I've resigned myself to not feeling anything anymore, being calm and measured the way I am. As if I was somehow bettering the world when I was freaked out by everything I heard on the news, and I really mean everything. Back then I was so anxious I lived with perpetual nausea, and spent most of my days in a dizzy state or in bed, and I clenched my jaw so tightly it locked for months, because I couldn't figure it out. I just couldn't figure out how to live in this world.

    I do not think my anxiety when I was 20 helped anything. I don't think it motivated me to be better, to try harder. Though I do fear that we are all a little too calm about the threats facing our species and this planet, I fear more that we have all gotten so good at consuming the madness that it does not keep us up at night. Not that I want you to be up at night. I don't want to be there either. Yet, I also don't want to justify this as normal.

    This collection by Ramsay offers an opportunity to examine our parallels, hers decades before my generation's. Reading this caused me to wonder about the collective buildup of years of distress over threats we seemingly have no control over. It is remarkable how much of the fears and hopes our two generations share; it does cast a line in dark water to know that our mothers, our elders, have wisdom to draw on, and hold the same griefs we do. Perhaps with this understanding we can learn from one another, can share resources and knowledge and move with grace and wisdom as we address these challenges.

The world is loud, this is true. But there are no sirens yet, and this does worry me.

Reviews of:
The God Seed and The Dalai Lama's Wife

"A deep meditation into life's most elusive experiences, this book reflects on the questions, What is the nature of God? What is the nature of humanity? and, What is the nature of the relationship between the two?"
~Bradley Helliwell~

"This book is for those times when, because society's dysfunctions seem almost overwhelming, we need most to remember the good news ~ that each new day represents not one but an infinite number of opportunities to begin again, to make healthier choices, to see beauty, and to remember the light of our God Seed within. Remember too that The Woman is always there, in even those most challenging moments, and She holds Her Hand out to you yet."
~Dana & Lori~

"This book is beautiful, poetic and engaging. Like a smooth blend of tea, it slowly perfumes its way into the reader's mind. A rare read in this post-Renaissance era, as we now have the fortune to witness a spiritual subject and a good aesthetic reunited. God Seed is a karma where love for one becomes one for all."
~Leslie Luo~

"What a joy!!! I read into the darkness with my iPhone flashlight to finish it!"
~T. James~

www.ingramcontent.com/pod-product-compliance
Lightning Source LLC
Chambersburg PA
CBHW031452040426
42444CB00007B/1074